CHERRY'S MORECAMBE BAY

ALL PHOTOGRAPHS BY PETER CHERRY FRPS

Dedicated to Ced, Olive and Jean, and those who appear in both of my books but are sadly no longer with us, in particular Tony 'Tant' Wilson and his elder son Tony.

I would like to express my thanks to the people, and families of the people, who appear in this book, and to all at J. Salmon Ltd.

ISBN 978-0-9511404-6-8

Printed by J.Salmon Ltd., Sevenoaks, Kent.

www.jsalmon.co.uk

Published by Peter Cherry, whose publisher imprint is Peter Cherry (Lytham)

www.petercherry.com   and   www.morecambebay.com

CONTENTS

MORECAMBE BAY – MAPS

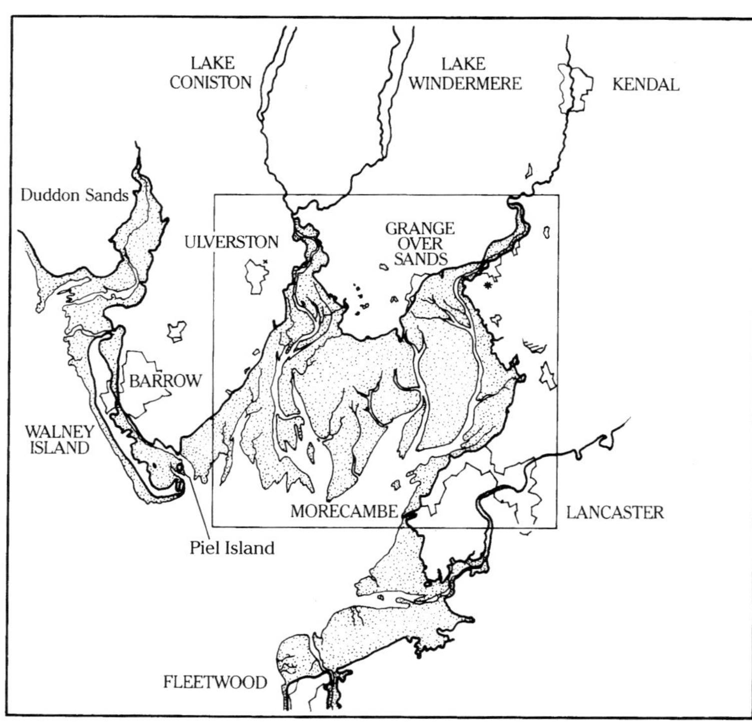

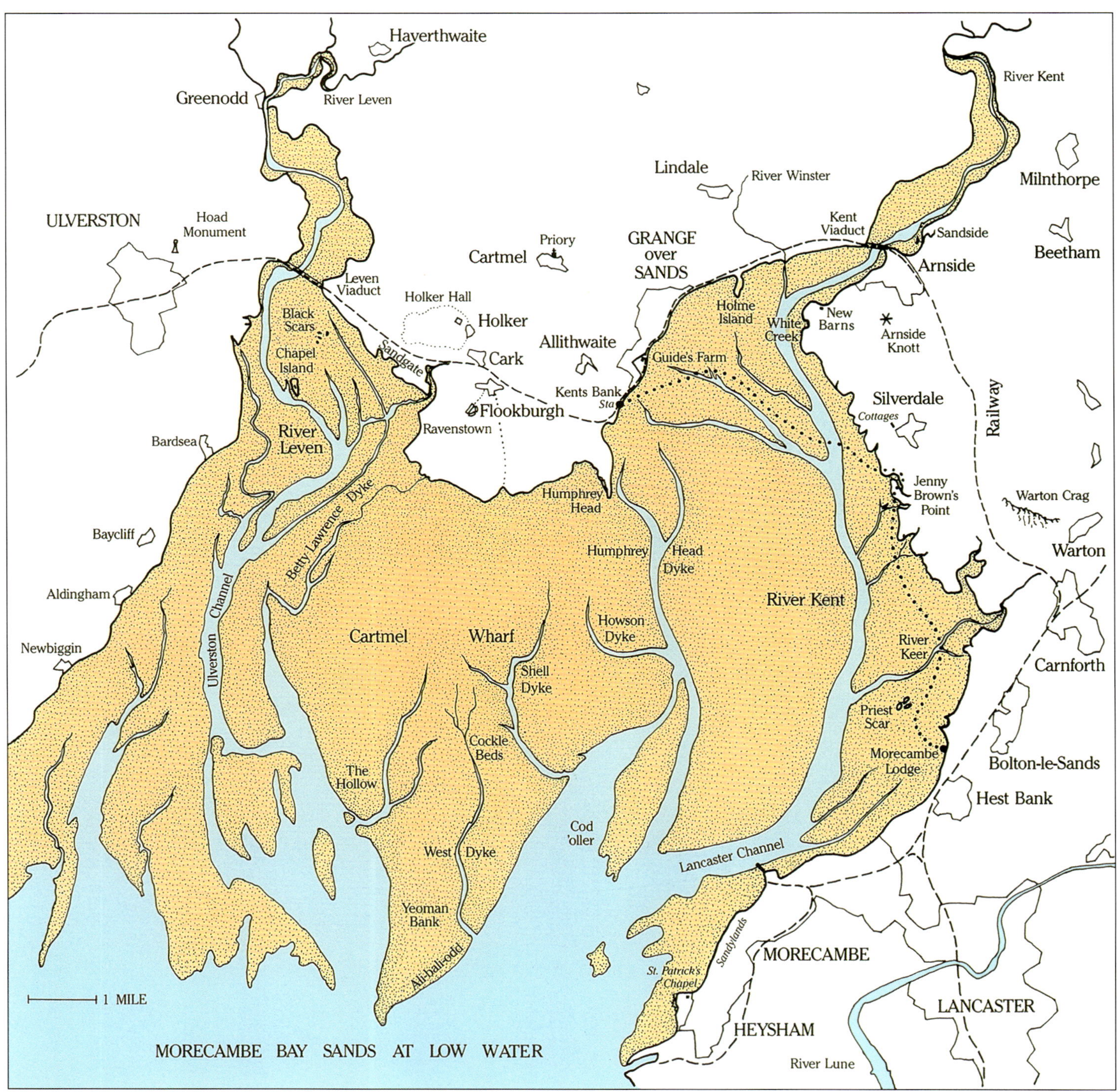

Haverthwaite
River Kent
Greenodd
River Leven
Lindale
River Winster
Milnthorpe
ULVERSTON
Hoad Monument
Cartmel
Priory
GRANGE over SANDS
Kent Viaduct
Sandside
Beetham
Leven Viaduct
Holker Hall
Arnside
Black Scars
Holker
Holme Island
White Creek
New Barns
Arnside Knott
Chapel Island
Cark
Allithwaite
Sandgate
Guide's Farm
Silverdale
Bardsea
River Leven
Flookburgh
Kents Bank
Sta
Cottages
Ravenstown
Railway
Baycliff
Humphrey Head
Jenny Brown's Point
Warton Crag
Humphrey Head Dyke
Warton
Aldingham
Betsy Lawrence Dyke
River Kent
Ulverston Channel
Newbiggin
Cartmel
Wharf
Howson Dyke
River Keer
Carnforth
Shell Dyke
Cockle Beds
Priest Scar
The Hollow
Morecambe Lodge
Bolton-le-Sands
Hest Bank
Cod 'oller
West Dyke
Lancaster Channel
Yeoman Bank
Sandylands
MORECAMBE
Ali-ball-oddi
St. Patrick's Chapel
LANCASTER
1 MILE
HEYSHAM
MORECAMBE BAY SANDS AT LOW WATER
River Lune

THE EVER CHANGING BAY

Morecambe Bay is a remarkable part of the north-west coastline of England. Its 120 square mile sands are revealed twice every 24 hours by the outgoing tide. After the tide ebbs, people venture onto the sands to make their living or simply enjoy the unique scenery when guided by Cedric Robinson; on foot or in horse drawn carriages, as in the pictures above and opposite.

The famous carriage crossing of Morecambe Bay, led by HRH The Duke of Edinburgh on May 30, 1985, with his four-in-hand carriage guided by Cedric Robinson, sitting alongside him.

Crossing the channel of the River Kent, which runs through Morecambe Bay. The Duke of Edinburgh's four-in-hand carriage is on the far left of the picture.

The limestone silhouette of Humphrey Head, as seen From White Creek, near Arnside. It is said that the last wild wolf in England was shot on Humphrey Head.

Cottages on the shore of Silverdale, Lancashire. The Cumbria – Lancashire border runs east to west between Silverdale and Arnside.

The snow covered Lakeland mountains, seen from Hest Bank, just north-east of Morecambe town.

The mile long sea wall, which stretches out from Jenny Brown's Point, near Silverdale.

The shimmering silver sands of Morecambe Bay – a world like no other.

CEDRIC, THE SANDS GUIDE

Cedric Robinson was appointed to the ancient post of Queen's Guide To The Sands Of Morecambe Bay in 1963 and has since guided many hundreds of thousands of walkers safely across. Even though Cedric was preceded by 24 Sands Guides, going back to the year 1548, it is he who has made the post of Sands Guide nationally and internationally famous.

Cedric's home, which comes with his job, is Guide's Farm in the west of Grange Over Sands and was built prior to 1548 when the Duchy of Lancaster created the post of Sands Guide. The farm's land covers about eleven acres in total and is triangular in shape, with the apex of the triangle at the top of a steep hill. It is said that Oliver Cromwell once slept there in the days when the house offered ale and an overnight stay to travellers who crossed the sands from the south shore, some eight miles away.

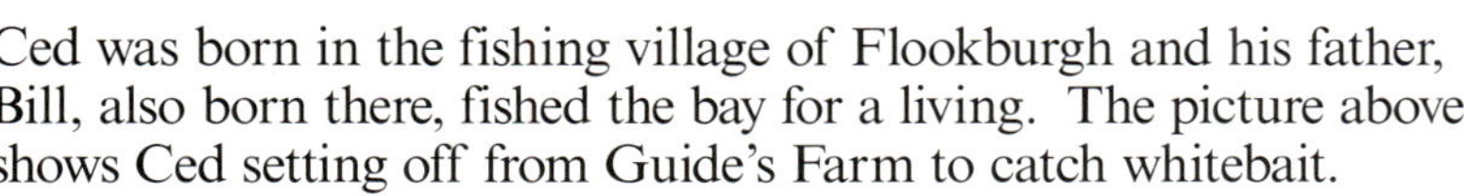

Ced was born in the fishing village of Flookburgh and his father, Bill, also born there, fished the bay for a living. The picture above shows Ced setting off from Guide's Farm to catch whitebait.

The tiny whitebait fish.

Ced pulls in the whitebait net.

Guide's Farm in winter, seen from the slope of its fields looking across part of the bay to the hill that is Arnside Knott – which can be seen to the right of the picture. Snow and ice covers the foreshore.

The meadow of Guide's Farm in mid-summer, looking towards Arnside and Silverdale. The large ash tree on the left has since blown down in a severe gale.

Guide's Farm by day and by night. The attached barn on the left is traditionally not whitewashed.

Ced's father, Bill, comes to visit Ced and his wife Olive at Guide's Farm, and lights his pipe. He lived to be 102 years old, from 1904 to 2006, so Ced expects to be doing his guide's job for some years to come, if he has inherited his father's longevity.

THE FLOOKBURGH SHRIMPERS

A shrimping trip, out from Flookburgh, with 'Tant' Wilson driving, next to him elder son Tony, and on the trailer, younger son Michael. Tractors replace fishing boats on this side of the bay – small boats are used on the southern Morecambe town side. This photograph appears both simple and timeless, and is one of the best photographs I have ever taken.

Tant stretches a shrimp net into the starting position. When being pulled behind a trailer, in turn towed by the tractor, the shrimp nets cause the shrimps to jump over the steel bar along their bottom edge, so that the shrimps are swept into the fine mesh. Each trailer will usually pull a pair of such nets, as seen in the lower picture.

A shrimp trawl in progress. Tant says to me 'I don't start to worry until the water level gets close to the air intake of the tractor'!

Tant whistles a tune while he and his son Tony wait patiently during a trawling session, which might last the best part of an hour. Tant afterwards strains with a heavy net full of brown shrimps – they only become the familiar pink colour after boiling.

Tant drives at speed, through channels both shallow and deep to reach the cockling grounds.

Tant and Michael rock the jumbos – planks of wood with handles used to bring the cockles to the surface. Les and Tony flick the revealed cockles into hand nets using three pronged forks called crambs.

Tony blows steam off the newly boiled shrimps to see their colour and gauge if they are ready. The shrimps are cooked in a hemispherical iron cauldron heated by a central-heating burner.

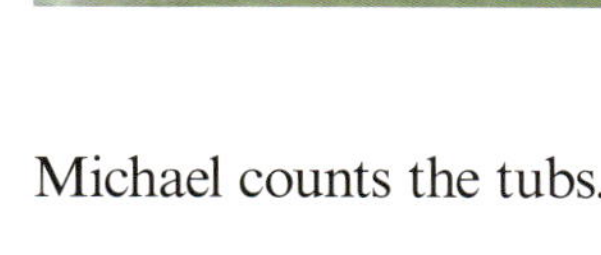

Michael counts the tubs.

'Potting' is carried out by spooning hot, liquid, butter onto shrimps in the famous plastic tubs which sell right around the UK, and abroad. This is Agnes.

FOLLOWING THE SANDS

Making a living from fishing in Morecambe Bay was, and is, known as 'following the sands'. Ced and his daughter Jean set the hazel stakes used to hold the fluke nets. Ced first works a pilot hole into the sand using the iron rod he is holding in his right hand. The stakes are then hammered in, and the netting tied on.

Flukes are a type of flat fish similar to plaice and gave the village of Flookburgh its name. Ced's helpers wash the flukes in a shallow pool.

Ced disentangles a mature fluke from the net, his hair swept by the bitter wind.

Setting off, to drive to a second fluke net. The tractor engine is left turning over all the time, as an engine which will not restart can present a danger, when the tide flows again.

Jean, Ced and two friends work at the second fluke net.

Disentangling a fluke quickly, takes years of practice.

Ced's wife, Olive, looks out of Guide's Farm's front window to see Ced returning.

CEDRIC'S CROSS BAY WALKS

The beginning of a cross bay walk in high summer, from Hest Bank on the Morecambe town side of the bay. Each walk can attract several hundred people, and various charitable groups often join in to raise money for their causes.

Setting off on the eleven mile cross bay walk, heading first for Jenny Brown's Point, near Silverdale.

Michael from the Kents Bank Post Office store, talks with Ced.

Ced keeps continual watch over his followers, keeping an eye
out for any recently moved quicksand.

My parents, Ian and Rosemarie, on the cross bay walk.

My sister, Monica, with wet dogs
Matt and Josh.

Heading out from rocks, after the halfway stop at Jenny Brown's
Point, now setting course for the water channel cut into the sands
by the River Kent.

Ced strides out, now wearing a sweater because of the cool winds in the middle of the bay.

Three boys and a man with an Arabic head-dress smoking a cigar! Have you spotted the man in the overalls also. This shows there are 'all sorts of people' joining the cross bay walks!

Crossing the channel of the River Kent, in the bay, just beyond halfway. On some walks the water level can reach the bottom of an adult's shorts. This happens when the River Kent has been swollen by heavy rain in the previous one or two days. After very heavy rain for several preceding days, Ced sometimes has to cancel a walk due to a dangerously deep river channel.

Heading for Kents Bank on the 'home stretch'.

Arriving at the cross bay walk finishing point, of the railway station at Kents Bank – to the right.

HARVESTING COCKLES

Chris pours cockles into a basket, while Ced rocks the jumbo to bring the cockles to the surface.

Ced continues to operate the jumbo, then flicks the cockles into a hand net using a cramb.

Ced cockling with his daughter, Jean and two friends.

Chris uses a small rake, which gathers the cockles faster than a cramb.

BOATS AND BIRDS

The end of a cold winter's trip from Piel Island – in the distance – to Roa Island. The remains of Piel Castle can clearly be made out. The tiny Piel Island is just above the southern tip of Walney Island, and can be found on my map on page 4.

This wreck is near the mouth of the River Lune, which flows into Morecambe Bay through Lancaster.

A flock of oystercatchers, which are plentiful on the bay.

This is a large flock of small wading birds, probably dunlin or knot, wheeling and swirling in a breathtaking synchronised display, so characteristic of the bay, particularly in the colder months.

PEOPLE OF THE BAY

Jean's former brother in law, Mark, shepherding.

Ced's father, Bill, who lived to be 102 (1904 – 2006)

Amy, Jean's daughter and Ced's granddaughter.

Michael Wilson with a pony in Flookburgh.

A summer carnival in Allithwaite, a village close to the bay – see my map on page 5.

SUNRISE

A winter's morning at Arnside, looking towards Grange Over Sands.

An icy winter's morning at New Barns, looking towards Holme Island.

A boy paddles slowly, during a misty morning on the River Kent estuary, at Arnside.

On the shore opposite Morecambe town promenade in early morning.

DAYTIME

Hest Bank in summer, and close to the starting point of the cross bay walks. The roaming sheep feed on salt marsh grass, which is said to give their meat a much sought after flavour – and fetch a premium price. Grange Over Sands is visible in the distance.

Thousands of sea-pink flowers on the Hest Bank salt marsh, so characteristic of the bay in high summer.

A mercurial sand landscape, sculpted twice a day by the ebbing tide.

At the very heart of the bay, about four miles from the shore.

The village of Arnside became popular with visiting Victorians, after the railway was laid around the bay in the late 1850's. The white building on the right was once a wealthy person's private house, but became one of two village pubs; The Albion.

When I was very young my father told me that these two trees 'knotted together' gave the hill above Arnside on which they stand, its name; The Knott. This photograph was taken some years ago and I believe that little now remains of this once famous landmark. The ashes of both of my 'Cherry' grandparents were scattered here, as they lived in Arnside for many years and loved the area.

This is the River Lune, which is one of the three main rivers flowing into Morecambe Bay. The other two principal rivers flowing into the bay are the River Kent, which flows through Kendal, and the River Leven, which flows out from the southern tip of Lake Windermere. The River Keer and the River Wyre also flow directly into the bay. The River Bela flows into the River Kent estuary.

This is the promenade in the town of Morecambe, which is the home to many family-run hotels. It is also a perfect location for photographers who want to capture world-class sunsets.

The River Kent estuary at Arnside, in winter.

The shore near Siverdale, in winter.

This is the ancient church of St Peter's in Heysham village, on the edge of the bay, where I was Christened. This church was built on the site of an earlier Saxon church.

The ancient graves at St Patrick's Chapel, Heysham – next to St Peter's Church – which were hewn out of solid rock. Archaeology has shown there was human activity in the area where the graves now stand, about 12,000 years ago.

A remarkable corner of England, which I have known all my life.

A view from the western side of the bay, looking towards Roa Island, in the distance.

A limestone outcrop near the shore at Silverdale.

A tree which is so characteristic of the bay, swept into shape by the localised winds, usually blowing onto land from the sea's surface.

SUNSET

New Barns at Arnside, a bay within a bay. Holme Island is on the right, with Grange Over Sands in the distance.

A view from Arnside, looking down the estuary, towards the mound of Kirk Head.

The remains of a baulk trap used to catch a wide variety of fish, many years ago. The upright posts seen in the picture were once interwoven with thin hazel sticks to make two sides of a V shaped 'fence' which would funnel fish into a smaller mesh net, when the tide ebbed.

Morecambe Bay, which largely faces west, is famous for its sunsets, which are a match for those anywhere in the world.

Digging for bait worms, on the shore opposite Morecambe town promenade.

A dream landscape, like no other.

The Silverdale salt marsh. Not a place to be walking at night - because it is a maze of small channels and pools – as I once did while taking photographs late in the day.

Piel Island is on the left horizon, with Roa Island on the right horizon, photographed on a crystal clear evening.

No two sunsets over Morecambe Bay are ever the same, and each one can change in the few seconds it takes to wind one's film on for the next photograph.

Just out from the Sandylands promenade in Morecambe town, there is a strange type of walled enclosure forming a one foot deep pool. I can only think that this was, at one time, provided for children to paddle in, or possibly sail model boats in.

This is the best sunset photograph I have ever taken, and is used on the cover of this book. It was taken a couple of hundred yards out from Morecambe town promenade, on a cold still, December evening. I was experimenting with 3D photography when taking this shot, which involved two identical cameras mounted together and fired simultaneously.

An idyllic view, near the Silverdale shore.

A view from Arnside Knott towards Humphrey Head – on the right.

A view from the Morecambe town side of the bay, towards the Cumbrian hills.

This is the shore near Morecambe town promenade. I have never taken any photograph through a coloured filter – as I explain on the back cover of this book.

The rocks on part of the Heysham shoreline.

TWILIGHT

Moonrise over Morecambe Bay. I took this photograph while out with Ced, cockling, using the handle of a jumbo as an improvised tripod. This allowed me to use the slow shutter speed required in the very low light conditions, and still get a sharp photograph.

A darker mood. The ancient graves cut into solid rock, at St Patrick's Chapel, Heysham. These were partly filled with rainwater when the photograph was taken, adding to the eeriness . The ruins of the adjacent chapel itself, date to the 8th or 9th century.

From White Creek, looking towards Holme Island and the lights of Grange Over Sands.

A brack, or break-away in the sands, near Silverdale. Humphrey Head can be seen on the horizon.

A serene view, not far from the baulk trap remains, which I described in the previous chapter.

This is a view from the Silverdale shore, looking towards Humphrey Head. Morecambe Bay is unique, and everyone in the UK should visit it, as well visiting the better known – and nearby – Lake District. I hope that this book has encouraged you to explore the Morecambe Bay area, and perhaps join in on one of Cedric Robinson's famous cross bay walks. Please visit my two websites listed on the back cover for further details.

THOUGHTS AND MEMORIES

Peter Cherry with Cedric Robinson in the mid 1980's during a cross bay walk.

A tractor and trailers used to carry official photographers alongside the carriages crossing the bay on 30 May 1985.

I have published this book myself in order to have total creative control of photograph selection, cropping and layout, which are not usually carried out by the photographer, when books of photos are published, but which I consider to be essential final steps in the artistic process, starting when the shutter release button is pressed.

I was born in the seaside town of Scarborough, Yorkshire, in 1959 and first used my father's Olympus half frame camera, loaded with colour slide film, when I was about 9 years old. In 1977 I attended Lancaster University, close to Morecambe Bay, to do a degree in Mechanical Engineering during which time I often took photographs around the bay using an Olympus OM1 camera. After university, I joined Ilford Photo in Mobberley, Cheshire, as a Design & Development Engineer. In 1986 aged 27, I published my first book myself, entitled 'On Morecambe Bay' using photographs I had taken over the previous nine years. In 1995 I decided to leave work and become self employed, which I am to this day, and now earn part of my living working as a professional photographer.

I would like to record a list of people (in no particular order) who are, or have been, important in my life. My family: Mum and Dad, Monica, Grandma, Grandfa, Oma, Trudel, Minni, Barbel, close friends Ced, Olive and Jean, school friends, David Drewett, Donald Clark, work friend Dave Aspaturian and wife Karen, Andrew Brown, and Chris Buck.

Please visit my two websites: www.morecambebay.com which will tell you how to join future cross bay walks, and let you view free video clips about Cedric Robinson's life, and www.petercherry.com where you can download the edited text of my first book 'On Morecambe Bay' free of charge.